The Rescue
of the
Thrift Industry

Studies in the Regulation of Economic Activity
TITLES PUBLISHED

Studies in the Regulation of Economic Activity

The Rescue
of the
Thrift Industry

A Staff Paper by Andrew S. Carron

THE BROOKINGS INSTITUTION
Washington, D.C.

© 1983 by
THE BROOKINGS INSTITUTION
1775 Massachusetts Avenue, N.W., Washington, D.C. 20036
ISBN 0-8157-1301-0
Library of Congress Catalog Card Number 83-71590

1 2 3 4 5 6 7 8 9

THE BROOKINGS INSTITUTION is an independent organization devoted to nonpartisan research, education, and publication in economics, government, foreign policy, and the social sciences generally. Its principal purposes are to aid in the development of sound public policies and to promote public understanding of issues of national importance.

The Institution was founded on December 8, 1927, to merge the activities of the Institute for Government Research, founded in 1916, the Institute of Economics, founded in 1922, and the Robert Brookings Graduate School of Economics and Government, founded in 1924.

The Board of Trustees is responsible for the general administration of the Institution, while the immediate direction of the policies, program, and staff is vested in the President, assisted by an advisory committee of the officers and staff. The by-laws of the Institution state: "It is the function of the Trustees to make possible the conduct of scientific research, and publication, under the most favorable conditions, and to safeguard the independence of the research staff in the pursuit of their studies and in the publication of the results of such studies. It is not a part of their function to determine, control, or influence the conduct of particular investigations or the conclusions reached."

The President bears final responsibility for the decision to publish a manuscript as a Brookings book. In reaching his judgment on the competence, accuracy, and objectivity of each study, the President is advised by the director of the appropriate research program and weighs the views of a panel of expert outside readers who report to him in confidence on the quality of the work. Publication of a work signifies that it is deemed a competent treatment worthy of public consideration but does not imply endorsement of conclusions or recommendations.

The Institution maintains its position of neutrality on issues of public policy in order to safeguard the intellectual freedom of the staff. Hence interpretations or conclusions in Brookings publications should be understood to be solely those of the authors and should not be attributed to the Institution, to its trustees, officers, or other staff members, or to the organizations that support its research.

242241

Foreword

THE THRIFT industry in the United States has been both the beneficiary and the victim of extensive government intervention in financial markets. Landmark legislation of the early 1930s promoted the thrifts— savings and loan associations and mutual savings banks—as principal conduits for home mortgage funds and consumer deposits. Benign regulation and a prosperous economy fostered the rapid growth of the thrift institutions in the 1950s and 1960s. These same regulations, however, led to stagnation in the late 1970s and the threat of insolvency in the 1980s. In 1982 the federal government decided to remove itself from many aspects of price and service regulation in the thrift industry. That decision provided the impetus for the recuperation of the industry.

The developments that led to the recent crisis were analyzed in Andrew S. Carron's *The Plight of the Thrift Institutions*, published by Brookings in early 1982. At that time, the industry's outlook was bleak. However, lower interest rates after mid-1982, combined with new government policies, rescued the thrifts from possible collapse. This staff paper updates and extends the material presented in the earlier study, analyzes the legislative changes made in 1982, and assesses the industry's prospects in light of those initiatives and current economic conditions.

Andrew S. Carron is a senior fellow in the Brookings Economic Studies program. He acknowledges the helpful comments on earlier drafts provided by his Brookings colleagues Barry P. Bosworth and Anthony Downs, and by Frederick E. Balderston, Kent W. Colton, and Richard W. Kopcke. The author is also grateful to Joy O. Robinson for research assistance and Kathleen Elliott Yinug for secretarial assistance. Carol Rosen edited the manuscript, and Penelope Harpold verified its factual content.

This is the twenty-first publication in the Brookings series of Studies in the Regulation of Economic Activity. The series presents the results of research on public policies toward business. The study was funded by grants from the Ford Foundation, from the Alfred P. Sloan Foundation, and from the Alex C. Walker Educational Fund and Charitable Foundation.

The views expressed here are those of the author and should not be ascribed to the foundations whose assistance is acknowledged above or to the trustees, officers, or other staff members of the Brookings Institution.

BRUCE K. MAC LAURY
President

March 1983
Washington, D.C.

THE THRIFT industry approached collapse in 1982. Operating losses and deposit outflows came close to exhausting the regulatory agencies' capacity to keep the savings institutions afloat. At that point, massive federal intervention, akin to nationalization of the industry, would have been required to protect depositors and maintain stability in financial markets. That would have destroyed the independent identity and long-run viability of the savings and loan associations and mutual savings banks. Individual institutions may have survived, but not the industry. The direct costs of government assistance and the indirect costs associated with the dismantling of established credit relationships would have been great.

This crisis was resolved by a potent combination of lower market interest rates, engineered by the Federal Reserve Board, and landmark legislation, for which many can share credit. Few realize how close the thrifts came to complete disarray; fewer still appreciate the difficulty of the challenges ahead. Substantial failures can be expected in the next few years, from both the lingering effects of the 1980–82 crisis and the inability of some thrifts to adapt to the new, less regulated environment.

This staff paper is an account of the industry's recent performance and the rescue operation mounted by the agencies and Congress. It also explores the prospects for the thrift institutions. The projections are based in part on a revised version of the model used in an earlier study,[1] so a comparison of the revised and the original projections should illustrate some of the opportunities and pitfalls inherent in such an exercise.

The Performance of the Thrift Industry in 1982

Despite a more favorable economic and regulatory climate after midyear, the pattern observed in 1981—of negative operating income leading to declining net worth and consolidation through merger—

1. Andrew S. Carron, *The Plight of the Thrift Institutions* (Brookings Institution, 1982).

1

continued unabated through 1982. Operating losses exceeded the record levels of the previous year, and the number of firms declined dramatically. Among the 4,002 federally insured savings and loan associations in operation at the end of 1980, there were 843 disappearances over the ensuing two years. During the same period, 184 firms began operation, bringing the total in operation to 3,343.[2] The number of mutual savings banks fell from 463 in 1980 to 424 by the end of 1982.[3]

In part, this decline was simply the consequence of earlier events. To a substantial degree, however, the economic and policy environment in 1982 contributed to the thrift industry's problems.[4]

Operating Environment

Interest rates remained at exceptionally high levels during the first half of 1982, reversing a modest decline observed at the end of 1981. The six-month Treasury bill rate fluctuated in the range of 12.2 to 13.7 percent between January and July 1982, compared with an average rate of 11.5 percent in December 1981.[5] Rates on longer-term issues remained well above short-term rates as a steep yield curve was established. These were the results of the restrictive monetary policy pursued by the Federal Reserve Board as a means of dampening inflation.

Thrifts were unable to attract and retain the retail deposits (under $100,000) that have been the core of their liability structure. Interest rate ceilings under regulations of the Depository Institutions Deregulation Committee (DIDC) continued to play a role in the liability structure of the thrifts. Ceiling rates on thirty-month small savers certificates exceeded 14 percent during the first half of 1982, and depositors shifted funds to those accounts. Because market-rate low-denomination short-term accounts were not available through most of 1982, depositors sought alternatives such as money market mutual

2. Federal Home Loan Bank Board, "Savings and Loan Activity in January," March 3, 1983, and previous issues (hereafter "S&L Activity"); and FHLBB, unpublished data, 1983.

3. National Association of Mutual Savings Banks (NAMSB), unpublished data, 1983.

4. A more detailed description of the industry's performance may be found in Michael J. Moran, "Thrift Institutions in Recent Years," *Federal Reserve Bulletin*, vol. 68 (December 1982), pp. 725–38; and Stephen T. Zabrenski, "Association Earnings: First Half of 1982," *Federal Home Loan Bank Board Journal* (December 1982), pp. 15–17.

5. Federal Reserve Board, statistical release G.13, October 5, 1982, and previous issues.

funds. Higher interest rates available outside the regulated depository institutions and, perhaps, concerns over the viability of the thrift institutions contributed to deposit outflows.

Deposit inflows to thrift institutions had been $6 billion in 1980. Flows then turned negative for virtually every month from the beginning of 1981 through November 1982, totaling −$39 billion in 1981 and −$29 billion during the first eleven months of 1982.[6]

Deposit runoffs and other cash outflows were accommodated by a large increase in borrowing. Federal Home Loan Bank System advances to savings and loan associations and private borrowing increased by $14 billion during the first eleven months of 1982 to peak at $102 billion.[7] Part of this growth represents retail repurchase agreements, accounts functionally similar to short-term deposits but not subject to interest rate ceilings or deposit insurance.

In July 1982 the Federal Reserve Board began implementing a monetary policy that would reduce market interest rates. This action was intended to foster a recovery from the recession and may have been motivated in part by concerns over the fragility of depository institutions.[8] Whatever the reasons, the Federal Reserve achieved its intentions: the six-month bill rate fell to 8 percent by year-end. Long-term interest rates declined as well, although not as far.

The change prompted depositors to alter their investment patterns. Balances in older fixed-rate certificates—those issued primarily between 1970 and 1978 for terms of up to eight years, yielding 6 to 8 percent—dropped by more than half, and there was no growth in the share of accounts with maturities of one year or less paying current market rates. By contrast, longer-term instruments at market rates increased substantially. (These include the small savers certificate and the new one-and-a-half-year retirement and three-and-a-half-year "no ceiling" instruments.) Longer-term market-rate deposits with maturities over one year increased from 18.7 to 27.4 percent of total deposits at savings and loans during 1982. At mutual savings banks, the share rose from 13.5 to 21.1 percent. This lengthening of liability maturities during a period of falling rates had an adverse impact on the outlook for the industry, as will be discussed later.

A new deposit instrument, initially offered in December 1982,

6. FHLBB, "S&L Activity"; NAMSB, unpublished data, 1983.
7. FHLBB, "S&L Activity."
8. See Andrew S. Carron, "Financial Crises: Recent Experience in U.S. and International Markets," *Brookings Papers on Economic Activity, 1982:2*, pp. 395–419.

partially reversed this pattern. The money market deposit account, authorized by the Garn–St Germain Depository Institutions Act of 1982, was the first to combine deposit insurance, liquidity, a market rate of return, and a low minimum denomination. It proved extremely popular. Account balances at thrifts reached $43 billion by the end of 1982, attracting $10 billion in new money, and that one month's influx reversed a third of the deposit outflows recorded between January and November.[9] For the year as a whole, though, deposit performance was disappointing.

Activity on the asset side of thrift balance sheets was sluggish as well. At the end of 1982, adjusted assets of the savings and loan industry totaled $691.9 billion, up from $602.4 billion at year-end 1980, a rate of increase that failed to keep pace with the economy as a whole.[10] Growth in the mutual savings bank industry was stagnant during the two-year period. Assets increased at a scant 0.8 percent annual rate to $174.2 billion by the end of 1982.[11]

Operating Results

Interest income on mortgage loans remained the largest component of gross earnings for the thrifts. Higher rates on new mortgages and the gradual repayment of lower-rate loans contributed to a continuing rise in interest income. Mortgage turnover averaged about 7 percent (an effective maturity of fourteen years for the average mortgage) at savings and loan associations throughout 1981 and most of 1982; by year-end, turnover had climbed to 10 percent in response to lower mortgage rates. In 1977 the turnover rate had been 14 percent (an effective maturity of seven years), reflecting economic growth and the more favorable gap between existing and new mortgage loans.[12] The slow turnover of old mortgages retarded the speed at which the

9. FHLBB, "S&L Activity"; NAMSB, unpublished data, 1983.

10. FHLBB, "S&L Activity." These and all subsequent data on savings and loan associations refer only to federally insured associations (87 percent of the firms and 98 percent of the assets in the industry). Data for 1982 have been adjusted to exclude appraised equity capital. Data for earlier years have been recomputed to reflect an accounting change in September 1982, which provides that certain balances previously reported as liabilities be reported as deductions from asset accounts.

11. NAMSB, unpublished data, 1983.

12. Turnover is mortgage loans repaid as a share of average mortgage loans held at insured savings and loan associations. Sales and purchases of mortgages and participations are excluded. The data are author's calculations based on FHLBB, "S&L Activity."

Table 1. *Selected Interest Rates, 1976–82*

Percent

Year	Rate on new mortgages[a]	Asset yield		Three-month Treasury bills[b]	Cost of funds	
		Savings and loan assns.	Mutual savings banks		Savings and loan assns.	Mutual savings banks[c]
1976	9.10	8.18	7.23	4.99	6.38	5.98
1977	9.02	8.44	7.43	5.27	6.44	6.03
1978	9.61	8.73	7.73	7.22	6.67	6.14
1979	10.89	9.29	8.26	10.04	7.47	6.80
1980	12.90	9.72	8.79	11.51	8.94	7.96
1981	15.00	10.11	9.42	14.08	10.92	9.48
1982	15.38	10.82	9.71	10.69	11.38	9.64

Sources: *Economic Report of the President, 1983*, p. 240; Federal Home Loan Bank Board, *Savings and Home Financing Source Book, 1981* (FHLBB, July 1982), pp. 56, 66; U.S. League of Savings Associations, *'81 Savings and Loan Sourcebook* (Chicago: USLSA, 1981), p. 41; National Association of Mutual Savings Banks, *1982 National Fact Book of Savings Banking* (New York: NAMSB, 1982), pp. 24, 27; and author's estimates based on unpublished data from FHLBB (1983), Federal Deposit Insurance Corporation (1983), and Mutual Savings Central Fund, Inc. (1983).

a. Effective interest rate on conventional first-mortgage loans originated by all major types of lenders for the purchase of previously occupied single-family homes.

b. Bank-discount basis.

c. Average annual interest rate paid on deposits.

industry's average return on assets approached market rates. The average return on total assets increased to 10.82 percent at savings and loan associations and 9.71 percent at mutual savings banks during 1982 (see table 1).

The largest expense was interest payments on deposits and other liabilities, which averaged 11.38 percent at savings and loan associations and 9.64 percent at savings banks. Operating expenses, which had been rising ahead of industry growth since the mid-1960s, continued to grow in relation to assets. The expense ratio for both savings and loans and mutual savings banks averaged 1.50 percent of assets during 1982 compared with 1.35 percent in 1980.[13]

Income taxes are carried on the income statement as an expense, but during the past few years thrift institutions have received refunds of previous taxes paid. Such receipts reduced savings and loan associations' after-tax losses by $1.5 billion in 1981 and $1.3 billion in 1982. For savings banks, net tax refunds over the period totaled $0.2

13. Author's estimates based on data in Zabrenski, "Association Earnings," p. 16, and FHLBB, unpublished data, 1983. The values for mutual savings banks were computed on a different basis in Carron, *Plight of the Thrifts*, pp. 13–14, and are therefore not directly comparable.

Table 2. *Profitability of the Thrift Institutions, 1961–82*

Retained earnings as percent of average total assets

Year	Savings and loan associations	Mutual savings banks
1961–65	0.80	0.45
1966–70	0.56	0.30
1971–75	0.65	0.47
1976	0.64	0.45
1977	0.79	0.55
1978	0.84	0.58
1979	0.68	0.46
1980	0.14	−0.12
1981	−0.75	−0.86[a]
1982	−0.65	−0.72[a]

Sources: NAMSB, *1982 National Fact Book,* p. 24; and author's estimates based on unpublished data from FHLBB (1983), FDIC (1983), and Mutual Savings Central Fund, Inc. (1983).

a. Adjusted to exclude capital infusions by FDIC in connection with assisted mergers.

billion.[14] Some institutions, however, have now received all the refunds for which they are eligible, so tax refunds will contribute less to the moderation of losses in the future.

As a result of these adverse factors, the thrift industry suffered losses of $5.6 billion during 1982—comparable to the $6.0 billion loss incurred in 1981 (see table 2). Net worth also continued to erode. By the end of 1982 the net worth of savings and loan associations had fallen to 3.51 percent of assets, a decline of 1.86 percentage points in two years.[15] For mutual savings banks, net worth was 5.30 percent of assets, a drop of 1.33 percentage points.[16]

The shift in the level and structure of interest rates since the late 1970s has been the principal cause of the thrifts' problems, of course,[17] both directly and indirectly. A comparison of 1980 and 1982 operating results for savings and loan associations will illustrate this point. During the second half of 1980, the last semiannual reporting period for which earnings were positive, the industry had net income of 0.10 percent of average assets (see table 3). For the first half of 1982, the semiannual

14. Carron, *Plight of the Thrifts,* pp. 13–14; and Zabrenski, "Association Earnings," p. 16.

15. Author's calculations based on FHLBB, "S&L Activity."

16. NAMSB, *1982 National Fact Book of Savings Banking* (New York: NAMSB, 1982), p. 6; and NAMSB, unpublished data, 1983.

17. Carron, *Plight of the Thrifts,* pp. 11–21.

Table 3. *Changes in Savings and Loan Operating Results, 1980–82*

Component of net income	Percentage of average assets[a]
Net income, base period, July–December 1980	0.10
Change from base period	−1.09
Change in return on assets less change in cost of funds	−0.75
Shift to longer-maturity deposits in falling-rate environment	−0.08
Effect of eroded net worth position	−0.11
Effect of change in operating expense ratio	−0.08
Effect of reduced tax loss carrybacks	−0.07
Net income, January–June 1982	−0.99[b]

Source: Author's estimates as described in the text based on Stephen T. Zabrenski, "Association Earnings: First Half of 1982," *Federal Home Loan Bank Board Journal,* vol. 15 (December 1982), pp. 15–17; and FHLBB, unpublished data (1982).

a. At annual rates.

b. An accounting change, the reclassification of certain liability items to contra-asset accounts, reduced reported net income by 0.02 percentage points to −1.01 percent of average assets.

period with the largest net loss, net income was −0.99 percent, a change of 1.09 percentage points. The direct increase in the cost of funds relative to the return on assets can account for fully 0.75 points of the deterioration in earnings. But other factors indirectly associated with interest rates contributed as well.

One indirect factor was a shift toward longer-term, higher-rate accounts, which prevented the thrifts from realizing immediately the full benefits of lower market interest rates. This shift in deposit mix caused 0.08 points of the recent loss. Second, the losses suffered by the industry in 1981 meant that there were relatively fewer assets on which to earn a return during 1982. Without the decline in net worth incurred in 1981, the rate of return in the first part of 1982 would have been increased by 0.11 points, all other things being equal. Third, as mentioned above, operating expenses increased relative to assets; had they grown no faster than assets since 1980, earnings would have been improved by 0.08 points. Finally, the depletion of tax refunds described earlier contributed 0.07 points to after-tax losses.[18]

These secondary factors contributed 0.34 percentage points to the decline in net income. Although the effect of current market interest rates dominates these indirect and lagged effects of the interest rate

18. The factors enumerated here total 1.09 percentage points and give the first-half 1982 net income according to the old definition (−0.99 percent). An accounting change that shifts some liability items to contra-asset accounts has the effect of increasing reported losses by 0.02 points to −1.01 percent of average assets.

environment, lower market rates alone will not completely resolve the problems of the thrift industry. This will become more apparent in the discussion of results from the forecasting model.

Analysis of the thrift industry often emphasizes changes in reported net worth. Assets and liabilities are reported at book value, however, thus obscuring the true earning power of various assets and the cost of liabilities. Calculation of the market value of assets and liabilities can provide a better—although still incomplete—picture of the industry's condition.[19] On this basis, net worth of the thrift industry has been negative since 1980. It did improve during 1982, however, from − $57 billion at the start of the year to − $40 billion at the end,[20] even though book-value net worth declined by $4 billion. This illustrates the favorable impact of lower interest rates and emphasizes the sensitivity of market-value calculations to changing economic conditions.

The superior information available from current-value data has led many firms in the thrift industry to adopt the technique for internal reporting. The Federal Home Loan Bank Board proposed that the industry report publicly on a current-value basis, but so far two obstacles have stood in the way.

First, more research needs to be done on both the computational methodologies and the reference index of current-value accounting. The earlier, simpler systems were easy to calculate but gave results that were overly sensitive to minor fluctuations in market interest rates. More complex techniques have been developed, but these obscure the links between management actions and observed results, thereby diminishing the feedback mechanism that is one of the major virtues of current-value accounting. Furthermore, the current value of the financial assets cannot be taken as the market value of the firm because appreciated nonfinancial assets and the value of the franchise are not included in the calculations.

The second difficulty is a procedural one. The thrift industry cannot adopt current-value accounting until the accounting profession and its standard-setting bodies agree to accept the practice. Such acceptance would necessarily imply application of the same rules to all financial institutions—banks and securities brokers, for example, as well as thrifts. And such broad acquiescence has been difficult to achieve.

19. Carron, *Plight of the Thrifts*, pp. 17–21.
20. Market-value net worth data are the author's calculations based on FHLBB, "S&L Activity"; NAMSB, *1982 National Fact Book*; and Federal Reserve Board, statistical release G.13.

Table 4. *Cash Flow Analysis for Federally Insured Savings and Loan Associations, January 1980–June 1982*

Billions of dollars

Factor	Jan.–June 1980	July–Dec. 1980	Jan.–June 1981	July–Dec. 1981	Jan.–June 1982
Lending activity					
Mortgage loans repaid	17.5	23.2	16.9	17.6	17.9
Mortgage loans closed	−25.7	−45.6	−29.7	−22.7	−21.7
Net loan sales	2.2	0.7	0.4	1.7	9.9
Net mortgage lending	−6.0	−21.7	−12.4	−3.4	6.1
Deposit activity					
New deposits received	204.3	219.8	222.9	259.1	258.3
Deposits withdrawn	−202.0	−211.5	−234.0	−273.4	−267.2
Net new deposits	2.3	8.3	−11.1	−14.3	−8.9
Cash income	28.4	29.8	32.0	34.6	35.9
Cash expense	−12.1	−13.0	−15.4	−18.0	−23.4
Increase in borrowing	−0.4	9.6	10.2	14.0	8.0
Net cash flow[a]	12.2	13.0	3.3	12.9	17.7
Liquid resources[b]	49.6	58.2	60.5	68.1	89.1
Cash flow + liquid resources	61.8	71.2	63.8	81.0	106.8
Exposure[c]	30.8	48.2	56.5	58.1	55.4
Liquidity ratio[d]	2.01	1.49	1.13	1.39	1.93

Source: Estimates based on FHLBB, "Savings and Loan Activity in December," January 28, 1983, and unpublished data.

a. Net mortgage lending, net new deposits, cash income and expense, and net borrowing.
b. Cash and securities (including mortgage-backed securities) in excess of regulatory minimum.
c. Private borrowing, uninsured jumbo certificates of deposit, and provision for future retail deposit withdrawals.
d. Cash flow plus liquid resources divided by exposure.

Liquidity

The earlier study of the thrifts suggested the possibility of a liquidity crisis.[21] That observation was based on industry cash flow to mid-1981. Subsequently the liquidity position of the savings and loan associations actually improved, even though deposit outflows increased (see table 4). This was accomplished initially through a reduction in new mortgage lending and later by the sale of mortgage loans into the secondary market. Substantial new borrowing also took place.

The measure of liquidity developed in the earlier study and refined here is the ratio of cash flow plus liquid resources to exposure. As shown in the table, this ratio declined from 2.01 to 1.13 before recovering to 1.93 by mid-1982. The institutions and their principal

21. Carron, *Plight of the Thrifts*, pp. 21–26.

lenders (the Federal Home Loan Banks) have shown their ability to adjust to deposit outflows and avoid serious liquidity problems.

Some FHLB advances are made to weak institutions to avert failures due to illiquidity. The Federal Savings and Loan Insurance Corporation guarantees repayment in such cases. Although the agency does not expect to incur losses under these arrangements, substantial amounts are involved. On average, over $500 million in FSLIC-guaranteed advances were outstanding during 1982.[22] In part, the problem of liquidity may have been avoided by shifting the consequences from the institutions to the federal regulatory agencies.

Concern over liquidity in 1981 and 1982 arose because of deposit outflows. Previous periods of disintermediation had been attributable to the higher interest rates available outside the regulated depository institutions.[23] Such flows were relatively predictable. But that explanation does not account for the much higher outflows at thrifts compared with banks. There appeared to be a slow and steady shift out of retail deposit accounts at savings and loan associations and savings banks to like accounts at commercial banks paying similar (or lower) interest rates. Regulators were unsure whether this runoff represented a loss of public confidence in the thrifts or simply reflected the wider array of services available at banks. The phenomenon was called the quiet run.

In 1982 small time and savings deposits at all depository institutions rose by $108 billion, and interest-bearing transaction accounts (NOW accounts) increased $24 billion.[24] Retail deposits at thrift institutions, however, grew only $43 billion compared with $89 billion at banks. These deposit components grew 15 percent at banks and only 7 percent at thrifts; that rate of increase—well below the average interest rate paid on deposits—indicates that all of the rise for thrifts is attributable to interest credited.

These are the consequences of a quiet run. But direct evidence of the phenomenon has proved elusive. The Federal Home Loan Bank Board commissioned a survey of public attitudes toward the thrifts, which was conducted in mid-1982. Granting the limitations of the

22. Federal Savings and Loan Insurance Corporation, "Comparative Statement of Condition" (FSLIC, 1983), note 9.
23. Disintermediation is the withdrawal of funds from financial intermediaries, such as thrift institutions.
24. Federal Reserve Board, statistical release H.6, February 18, 1983, and previous issues.

procedures used, the results offer no suggestion of a deterioration in public confidence.[25] Only 4 percent of the sample admitted to switching funds out of thrifts for reasons other than rates, which is insufficient to explain the observed shift in deposit balances between thrifts and banks. Conclusions on the existence of a confidence crisis await further analysis.

Government Policies toward the Thrift Industry

The government relied on existing supervisory and assistance techniques to support the thrift industry during the first half of 1982. There were indications by midyear that the limits on assisted mergers and liquidity lending were being reached.[26] The response was a less restrictive monetary policy and new legislation, even as mergers and limited capital assistance continued to be provided under preexisting authorities. Lower interest rates slowed the decline of the industry and lessened the drain on the deposit insurance funds, thereby ensuring the capacity of the existing system to cope with the ongoing problems. The new legislation permits a fundamentally new structure for the industry as well as the means of transition to that new structure. The Garn–St Germain Depository Institutions Act of 1982 enhanced the regulatory powers of the agencies, lessened asset and liability restrictions on thrifts, and mandated a further removal of deposit rate controls. By year-end the agenda for new thrift policies was completed. There remained but to see how successful the efforts would be.

Merger Policy

The principal means of resolving the earnings problems of individual thrifts has been and will continue to be merger. Regulators favor this approach because it conserves more of the assets of the insurance funds, at least over the near term, than alternative measures. Consolidation can cut fixed costs by reducing management duplication, closing redundant branch offices, and eliminating high-cost operators. Moreover, there is a value to an ongoing firm not reflected on the balance

25. Charlotte Chamberlain and Robert R. Shullman, "How Consumers See Thrifts: Safety, Rates, and Savers," *Federal Home Loan Bank Board Journal*, vol. 15 (September 1982), pp. 2–8.
26. See Carron, "Financial Crises," pp. 407–10.

sheet in the form of customer relationships, name recognition, and the possibility of geographic expansion. This value can be captured through a merger, thus reducing the costs to the regulatory agency.[27]

An advantage for the regulators that is less apparent is the ability to postpone recognition of assistance costs paid to the acquiring firm in a merger arrangement. Actual payment may be delayed, improving the regulatory agency's cash flow. Or the costs of aid may be made contingent on the future course of interest rates, in which case only part of the liability is shown on the balance sheet. The FSLIC, on which the greatest burden has fallen, is an on-budget agency. In the context of a governmentwide effort to reduce spending, the FSLIC has been under pressure to minimize reported outlays. One effect of a merger is to spread the industry's net worth more widely, delaying if not eliminating the impact on the insurance funds.

Any of several different types of merger may occur to deal with a failing thrift. A firm that has a relatively high net worth but that has incurred substantial losses because of excessive operating costs or an inability to attract new capital may be an attractive candidate for acquisition. The resulting voluntary merger can preempt supervisory intervention by an agency. The management of the failing firm has an incentive to arrange a voluntary merger to preserve its own position. Many of the apparently voluntary combinations over the past two years have occurred under such circumstances. The current rate (240 in 1981 and 244 in 1982) is more than double the rate of voluntary mergers in the late 1970s.

In supervisory mergers, the regulatory agencies (the FSLIC or the Federal Deposit Insurance Corporation) compel the operational and managerial changes necessary to make the failing firm attractive to an acquiring firm, but they do not provide financial assistance. During 1981, 61 savings and loan associations with assets of $3.9 billion disappeared through supervisory mergers. During 1982, 192 firms with assets of $22.2 billion were merged by this procedure.

The average failing firm involved in a voluntary or supervisory merger during the past two years has had assets of $100 million,

27. "In effect, we are selling market entry rights for the benefit of FSLIC. . . . Now this is a sticky business, but when faced with the alternative of draining the fund, most everyone has resigned themselves to the wisdom of this approach." Paper presented by H. Brent Beesley, director of the FSLIC, at the California Savings and Loan League Management Conference, San Diego, March 3, 1982, p. 7.

substantially smaller than the industry mean. These unassisted mergers are facilitated by the small size of the firms being acquired. Such tactics have generally not proved adequate for handling the problems of the large thrifts. For these, financial assistance from the regulatory agencies has been required. Twenty-seven savings and loan associations with assets of $11.6 billion were merged with assistance in 1981, and another seventy-seven with assets of $28.4 billion were merged in 1982.[28] The average size of these firms was more than $350 million, double the industry mean. There were three assisted mergers of mutual savings banks in 1981 and another eight in 1982.[29] Total assets of the eleven savings banks were $15 billion. The costs of this assistance have been substantial: approximately $1.0 billion for the FSLIC and $800 million for the FDIC in 1981; another $1.1 billion for the FSLIC and $1.0 billion for the FDIC in 1982.[30]

There is also a hybrid type of merger that the FSLIC has termed the phoenix plan. Where a number of failing thrift institutions are in the same geographic area, it has been difficult to find healthy and interested firms to acquire them, even when moderate amounts of assistance were offered. Often the failing firms have been relatively large and therefore costly to liquidate. These circumstances arose most frequently in New York State and in the Chicago area.[31] The FSLIC resorted to combining several failing firms into a new "phoenix" institution to operate under close agency supervision.[32] Cost reductions are achieved through elimination of excess management, boards of directors, and branches. The agency provides cash or notes in exchange for income capital certificates (debt-equity hybrids that lie between preferred stock and pure debt instruments in the hierarchy of creditors) to keep the firm's net worth above zero. Given this degree of assistance, the firm may eventually regain health or be merged into another with additional financial aid. Six such savings and loan associations have been formed—three in Illinois, two in New York, and one in Puerto Rico—representing approximately $20 billion in assets. Although the costs of these phoenix mergers have been small to date, the ultimate costs are not yet known.

28. These tabulations exclude the surviving firms in phoenix mergers (see below).
29. NAMSB and FDIC, unpublished data, 1983.
30. FSLIC and FDIC, unpublished data, 1983.
31. See Carron, *Plight of the Thrifts*, pp. 34–35, 84.
32. The surviving firm kept the name of one of the prior institutions.

Liquidation

The regulatory agencies see liquidation of an institution as a last resort. It is the most costly and cash- and time-intensive strategy. Only one thrift was liquidated in 1981 and one in 1982. The FSLIC also liquidated two savings and loan associations in the first quarter of 1983. Unlike bank liabilities, a significant share of which are not covered by deposit insurance, nearly all thrift liabilities would become obligations of the FSLIC or the FDIC in the event of a liquidation. Thus liquidation of a bank can be substantially less costly for the regulatory agencies than liquidation of a thrift of the same size. The closing of commercial banks and the payoff of their depositors are likely to continue at the rate of several a year, but thrift liquidations should be considered unusual events.

Regulators' Bill

The sharp increase in merger activity was a departure from earlier practice. Combinations approved in the interest of minimizing government assistance might have breached earlier standards for market concentration. Mergers among large firms in the same market and between associations in different states took place under the broad but vague statutes governing the FSLIC and the FDIC. That same legislation limited the ability of these agencies (particularly the FDIC) to provide support to ongoing firms. A proposal generally called the regulators' bill was assembled in 1981 to clarify the merger policy and liberalize the provisions for assistance. Reformulated as the Depository Insurance Flexibility Act, the regulators' bill became law as title I of the Garn–St Germain Act.

Congress established guidelines for mergers involving thrift institutions. The rules are generally consistent with recent regulatory practice, and substantial discretion remains with the agencies. Maintaining the integrity of the insurance funds takes precedence over other considerations. For example, the regulators must give preference to like-type and intrastate mergers over cross-industry and interstate combinations only when there is a tie bid for the smallest amount of assistance. Moreover, Congress granted certain new powers, including the right of federal agencies to compel the merger of state-chartered

14

institutions across state lines in contravention of state law. And the circumstances under which the FDIC can provide ongoing assistance were liberalized to correspond to the authority of the FSLIC.

Direct Assistance

During 1981 and 1982 many proposals were advanced to provide direct financial assistance to a broad segment of the thrift industry. Substantial differences existed in the depth and breadth of assistance, costs, incentives, and technical and political feasibility of the various plans. These coalesced as the Net Worth Certificate Act, title II of the Garn–St Germain Act. Although not as important over the long run as some other parts of the bill, this title provided the impetus for prompt enactment as the industry's condition deteriorated.

Under this measure, up to one-third of the thrift industry will be eligible to receive temporary financial assistance from the deposit insurance funds. To qualify, an institution must have net worth equal to 3 percent of assets or less and have incurred losses for the two previous quarters. (There are several other conditions, but these two are the most important.) The agencies are then authorized to exchange promissory notes of their own (like government agency securities) for net worth certificates (income capital certificates) issued by the institutions. This exchange boosts the net worth of the thrift even though no cash is involved in the initial transaction. There is a cash cost, however, as the agencies pay interest to the thrifts on the promissory notes, whereas interest (dividend) payments on the net worth certificates are not required unless and until the thrift returns to health. Congress authorized an assistance formula that begins with assistance equal to 50 percent of operating losses for firms with net worth between 2 and 3 percent of assets, escalating to 70 percent of operating losses when net worth falls below 1 percent. But the agencies have the discretion to vary the amount of assistance between zero and 100 percent of operating losses.

An important feature of this program is that it is permissive rather than mandatory for the regulators. And it involves an exchange of notes rather than an infusion of cash, which cushions the impact on the insurance funds. Theoretically, the agencies could issue an unlimited amount of promissory notes, receiving a like quantity of net worth certificates from the weak institutions to balance the accounts. In contrast, cash assistance could not exceed the current resources of

15

the insurance funds (Treasury securities plus authorized borrowing). The program as designed thus preserves cash for interest payments on the promissory notes and for merger assistance.

This program should not be seen as replacing assisted mergers, but rather as providing additional time for the regulatory agencies to arrange the further consolidation of the industry.[33] The FSLIC in 1982 faced more failures of savings and loan associations than it could handle, so a retardation in the rate of failures may have no effect on the rate of supervisory and assisted mergers. Nor does capital assistance imply an increase in the total costs of resolving the problems of the thrift industry. Firms that eventually return to health can repay the assistance with full interest. For those that ultimately fail, the promissory notes can fairly be characterized as a down payment on the assistance that would have been provided anyway.

In only a few cases will this new program represent an expansion of aid. These will be firms that would have merged unassisted but for the net worth certificate program. Instead they remain in operation, eventually begin showing positive profits, but never earn enough to pay current interest on their net worth certificates and do not reduce the principal owed. The likely costs of the assistance program will be reviewed in the section on the outlook for the industry.

Expanded Asset Powers

The savings and loan industry was resurrected in the 1930s and charged with promoting housing. To that end, associations were restricted in their investment and deposit-taking authorities. Their initial success and later deterioration in pursuing this strategy is well known, as are the many proposals over the years for reforming the asset and liability powers of thrifts.[34] Some reform was achieved in the Depository Institutions Deregulation and Monetary Control Act of 1980. The net worth assistance program provides modest transitory aid. But title III of the Garn–St Germain Act, the Thrift Institutions Restructuring Act, stands as the most fundamental reform of the thrift

---

33. See remarks of H. Brent Beesley in the *Washington Post*, October 12, 1982.

34. *The Report of the President's Commission on Financial Structure and Regulation* (Government Printing Office, 1971); *Financial Institutions and the Nation's Economy (FINE)*, Hearings before the Subcommittee on Financial Institutions Supervision, Regulation and Insurance of the House Banking, Currency, and Housing Committee, 94 Cong. 1 and 2 sess. (GPO, 1976); *The Report of the President's Commission on Housing* (GPO, 1982). See also Carron, *Plight of the Thrifts*, pp. 65–68.

industry since the Great Depression. The all-important commercial lending and demand deposit powers are extended to savings and loan associations for the first time. Loan-to-value and first lien restrictions on real estate loans are removed, and the limits on nonresidential real estate loans are raised. Savings and loans are given the authority to invest in one another's time deposits, in state and local securities, and in a wide variety of consumer loans. They may also engage in equipment leasing.

Many of these new investments may not exceed a specified percentage of assets—10 percent in the cases of commercial lending and leasing, for example. However, these constraints apply to all assets in the portfolio and not to new investments. Thrifts can devote a major share of new business to these activities without encroaching on the limits. At the current rate of asset growth for savings and loan associations (8.0 percent a year), nearly all net increases in assets for the average firm could go into just leasing and commercial loans for the next three years under existing legislation. And there is the strong possibility that Congress will eventually approve further liberalization of thrift powers.

Federal income tax laws are probably a more serious constraint on diversification. Thrift institutions can substantially reduce their tax burden if a specified portion of their assets is invested in mortgages and Treasury securities. For savings and loan associations, the required share is 82 percent and for savings banks, 72 percent. Eventually, Congress may amend the tax law to make the incentives consistent with the industry's new operating powers. And thrifts will find other means—tax-exempt securities, equipment leasing, and real estate—to reduce their tax rate. But, in the short term, savings and loan associations can retain their tax advantage and relax the constraint on investments by converting their charters to federal savings bank charters under title III of the Garn–St Germain Act. There was only one such conversion in 1982, but during the first quarter of 1983 fifty more applications for conversion had been filed with the FHLBB. State-chartered mutual savings banks can also convert to federal charters if they seek the same powers now accorded federal savings and loan associations.

Deposit Rate Ceilings

The Depository Institutions Deregulation Committee approved several new market-rate instruments on its own during 1982, but these

17

were insignificant in comparison with the money market deposit account (MMDA) mandated by Congress in title III of the Garn–St Germain Act. The sum of thrift deposits in new accounts other than the MMDA amounted to only $31 billion by the end of 1982, while the MMDA attracted $43 billion in the month of December alone.[35] The MMDA represents virtually the final removal of deposit rate ceilings after sixteen years in force.

One deposit instrument that held great promise in 1981 was the all savers certificate with its attraction of tax-exempt interest. Some estimated that sales would exceed $180 billion, although most disinterested analysts put the figure well below $100 billion.[36] Total sales by all depository institutions during the first year of the program amounted to only $53 billion.[37] Losses in the thrift industry were ameliorated by less than $500 million as a result of all savers certificates,[38] a noticeable but not decisive impact.

Deposit Insurance Reform

Title VII of the Garn–St Germain Act anticipates the need for reform of the deposit insurance system arising from the structural changes in the financial services industry. In particular, depository institutions will become more diverse, and some will choose to pursue higher risk/return strategies than others. A risk-based schedule for deposit insurance premiums would create incentives for prudent behavior, which do not exist in the current level-premium system. However, risk-related premiums might discourage innovation. Congress directed the three deposit insurance funds (the FSLIC, the FDIC, and the National Credit Union Share Insurance Fund) to undertake studies of the premium structure, the amount of coverage, and other elements of the current system and to present recommendations. Those reports were submitted in April 1983.

Late in 1982, however, the FSLIC proposed a new premium and rebate structure based on the interest-rate risk exposure of the institution. When the average maturities of an institution's assets and

35. The new accounts are seven-to-thirty-one-day accounts with $20,000 minimum, ninety-one-day money market certificates with $7,500 minimum, one-and-a-half-year no-ceiling retirement accounts, and three-and-a-half-year no-ceiling accounts. FHLBB, "S&L Activity," table 1; Federal Reserve Board, statistical release H.6.
36. Carron, *Plight of the Thrifts*, pp. 72–76.
37. FHLBB, "S&L Activity"; Federal Reserve Board, statistical release H.6.
38. Author's estimate.

liabilities differ, changes in market interest rates generate gains or losses.[39] The larger the discrepancy in maturities between assets and liabilities, the greater the risk. It is this aspect of savings and loan operations that the rate-sensitive premium was intended to address. Because of restrictions in the existing statutes, the proposed plan was somewhat crude and took no cognizance of other types of risk (for example, default). This administrative procedure may therefore provide the impetus for legislative changes.

The Outlook for the Thrift Industry

The forecasting model developed for the earlier study[40] was revised for this paper. More recent data and assumptions based on the events of 1982 were incorporated. Although the new projections follow a different path from that anticipated a year ago, the implications for industry structure and cost of assistance are not significantly changed.

Methodology

The forecasting model begins with data on the income, expenses, and financial condition of individual firms as of the most recent accounting period (calendar year 1981 for the results to be reported here). For savings and loan associations, the data cover 3,743 federally insured firms in operation at the end of 1981. This excludes 36 firms (less than 0.1 percent of the industry's assets) for which records were incomplete.

Within the model each component of assets and liabilities initially bears a rate of return specific to the firm. Assets and liabilities mature according to a schedule common to the industry but different for each item. For example, initially one-twelfth of outstanding mortgage loans are repaid annually; that fraction rises later to one-eighth as market rates are assumed to fall. Fixed-term liabilities turn over according to stated maturities. Reinvestment takes place at market rates, determining the path of gross income and cost of funds over time. Operating expenses are projected at a constant ratio to average assets. This permits the calculation of net income, which is then added to net worth (or subtracted in the case of a net loss).

39. See Carron, *Plight of the Thrifts*, pp. 12–18.
40. Ibid., pp. 27–38.

The change in deposit balances is set exogenously for the industry as a whole, and the pattern across firms is determined by historical experience. Increases in deposits above levels required for cash flow permit new investment, while deposit outflows generate additional borrowing. Cash flow and net income determine the growth in assets and liabilities.

The model generates income statements and balance sheets year by year and in equilibrium for each firm. The effects of any desired set of financial conditions and government policies can be simulated. The data can be analyzed for the entire industry or any part of it.

Determining viability. The model's primary objective is to measure the extent of structural change implied by recent events and the cost of regulatory assistance. For this a criterion of viability is required. As a first cut, firms are assumed not to be viable if net worth at book value is negative at the end of a forecasting year. Then some firms that still have positive net worth at the end of the forecasting period are found to have negative income in equilibrium even under the favorable environment for interest rates assumed for 1984 and beyond, and these too are considered nonviable. And finally there are associations that have positive net worth and positive net income in equilibrium, yet whose earnings are insufficient to pay even the interest due on the net worth certificates issued to the deposit insurers, as described earlier. Where such a subsidy of indefinite duration is implied, the firm is determined to be nonviable.

Yet not all nonviable firms will require government assistance. Many institutions that have high operating costs can return to profitability with the economies resulting from a voluntary merger. Marketing opportunities and other synergies may induce a large healthy firm to acquire a smaller weak firm without assistance. Where assistance is required, it is limited to that amount necessary for break-even operation of the acquired firm after cost-saving measures. This amount is therefore substantially smaller than the negative market value of the acquired firm might indicate.

Assumptions. Previous and current assumptions used in the model are shown in table 5.[41] The outlook for the economy is substantially different now from what it was a year ago. Interest rates initially moved higher rather than declining. Some favorable prospects (such as all savers certificates) failed to fulfill expectations. The outlook now

41. Note that the 1981 forecast relied on 1980 data and the forecast period ended with 1983.

Table 5. *Assumptions of the Forecasting Model, 1981–84*

Factor	1981	1982	1983	1984
Interest rates (percent)				
Mortgage contract rate				
1981 pessimistic forecast	14.0	14.8	13.5	. . .
Current forecast	14.4[a]	14.7[a]	13.7	13.3
Six-month Treasury bills				
1981 pessimistic forecast	14.3	13.8	12.8	. . .
Current forecast	13.8[a]	11.1[a]	9.4	9.4
Passbook accounts				
1981 pessimistic forecast	5.5	6.0	6.5	. . .
Current forecast	5.5[a]	5.5[a]	5.5	5.5
Annual growth in retail deposit balances (percent)				
1981 pessimistic forecast	3.2	9.8	9.8	. . .
Current forecast	1.1[a]	7.0[a]	11.7	11.4
Average all savers certificates outstanding (billions of dollars)				
1981 pessimistic forecast	12.2	44.4	13.3	0.0
Current forecast	4.2[a]	18.0[a]	3.3	0.0
Capital assistance program in effect				
1981 pessimistic forecast	no	no	no	no
Current forecast	no	no	yes	yes

Sources: Andrew S. Carron, *The Plight of the Thrift Institutions* (Brookings Institution, 1982), pp. 28–30; and author's estimates based on major private forecasters and the Congressional Budget Office.

a. Actual.

therefore is roughly comparable to that which was reported a year ago as the pessimistic forecast.

These assumptions are not intended to predict the course of interest rates. They merely represent a consensus of the major private econometric forecasting firms and the Congressional Budget Office as of late 1982.

Savings and Loan Associations

Industry performance is at the low end of the range previously anticipated, despite the recent decline in interest rates. Projections of the net income and the financial condition of federally insured savings and loan associations are in table 6. The 1981 forecast corresponds to the pessimistic forecast produced that year.[42] The current forecast in

42. Carron, *Plight of the Thrifts*, p. 30. Certain items have been recalculated to make the earlier data consistent with the FHLBB's new accounting treatment.

Table 6. *Forecast of Income and Financial Condition of Federally Insured Savings and Loan Associations, 1980–84*

	1981 pessimistic forecast	Current forecast	
		With net worth assistance	Without net worth assistance
Net income as share of average *assets (percent)*			
1980 (actual)	0.14	0.14	0.14
1981	−0.79	−0.76	−0.76
1982	−0.55	−0.65	−0.65
1983	−0.15	−0.04	−0.05
1984	. . .	0.51	0.50
Industry assets, end of year *(billions of dollars)*			
1980 (actual)	602.4	602.4	602.4
1981	647.1	640.4	640.4
1982	697.3	691.9	691.9
1983	757.9	760.2	759.0
1984	. . .	785.8	783.6
Net worth as share of assets, *end of year (percent)*			
1980 (actual)	5.37	5.37	5.37
1981	4.29	4.31	4.31
1982	3.47	3.51	3.51
1983	3.05	3.39	3.24
1984	. . .	4.09	3.81
Associations viable only with merger, *not receiving assistance*			
Number of institutions	451	475	492
Percent of institutions	11.3	11.9	12.3
Total assets (billions of dollars)	26.1	21.5	22.1
Associations not viable by 1984, *receiving merger assistance*			
Number of institutions	625	233	286
Percent of institutions	15.6	5.8	7.1
Total assets (billions of dollars)	83.4	60.8	69.9
Amount of assistance required (billions of dollars)	6.4	5.9	5.4

Source: Carron, *Plight of the Thrifts*, p. 30, for 1981 forecast, which does not include the effect of a net worth assistance program. Other data are author's estimates based on FHLBB, unpublished data (1982 and 1983). All data have been adjusted to reflect an FHLBB accounting change effective September 1982, which provides that certain balances previously reported as liabilities be reported as contra-assets (i.e., as deductions from asset accounts).

the center column includes the effects of FSLIC net worth assistance under the Garn–St Germain Act, while the final column assumes there is no such assistance.

The savings and loan industry reported a loss of $4.3 billion (0.65 percent of average assets) in 1982. Even this loss would have been greater but for substantial nonoperating income—gains on the sale of assets, for example. In both 1981 and 1982 more than 80 percent of the firms lost money. Operations will turn profitable during 1983, but a loss of 0.04 percent of assets will be recorded for the full year. According to the results of the model, 43 percent are forecast to record operating losses in 1983 and 15 percent in 1984. Net worth will dip to near 3 percent of assets before recovery begins. By that point, one-quarter of the firms will have net worth of less than 2 percent of assets. Net income from operations in 1984 will be 0.51 percent of average assets, or about $4 billion. Profitability should increase in subsequent years to a level of about 0.80 percent of assets.

As a result of losses between 1980 and 1983, substantial numbers of firms will not be viable over the long run. Most of these will merge without assistance. The number of such cases is put at 475 for the 1981–84 period, little changed from the 451 previously reported. Some associations will require assistance to merge, including forgiveness of their debts to the FSLIC. The number needing assistance is now estimated at 233, substantially fewer than the 625 projected earlier. The typical problem case is much larger in the later forecast, however, and costs of assistance are up. Merger assistance to weak savings and loan associations, previously estimated at $2.5 billion to $6.4 billion under alternative forecasts, is now projected to cost $5.9 billion—$4.9 billion in payments to acquiring firms and $1.0 billion in forgiven redemptions of net worth certificates (see below). These changes are partly the result of improvements in the structure of the model used to make the projections. Many small firms previously identified as requiring small amounts of assistance are now determined to be viable on their own or through a voluntary merger.

The industry's problems will reduce the number of firms by 708 from the 4,002 in existence at the end of 1980. There will continue to be large numbers of voluntary mergers motivated by reasons other than imminent failure; approximately 175 such combinations a year may be anticipated. At the same time, new associations continue to be chartered at a rate of about 100 a year. Thus by the end of 1984 there will probably be fewer than 3,000 federally insured savings and loan associations in the United States, a decline of more than 1,000 firms. These forecasts are in line with earlier predictions.

Capital assistance. Issuance of net worth certificates under the formula in the Garn–St Germain Act will improve the industry's performance over the short run. The results of the model indicate that the FSLIC could issue $1.22 billion in capital notes to as many as 816 associations in 1983; 258 of those firms plus another 19 associations would be eligible to receive additional assistance in 1984 totaling $250 million (net of repayments). With the return to profitability in 1985, net extensions of aid would be minimal. Eventually, $500 million of the $1.5 billion in notes would be redeemed with interest. The cash costs could reach approximately $130 million in 1983 and $150 million in 1984, with a present value cost of $1.0 billion over the ten-year life of the program.

As can be seen in table 6, the net worth assistance program can have its intended effect of increasing reported net worth. Industry earnings, however, would rise by only 0.01 percent of assets in 1983 and again in 1984, and the trend toward industry consolidation is little affected. The 708 mergers forecast to occur under the net worth assistance program are only 70 fewer than would occur without the program, an insignificant difference. There would have been more supervisory and assisted mergers in the absence of the program, but the costs of each assisted merger would have been less. Without the FSLIC's purchase of $1.5 billion in notes from the industry, a transaction that could ultimately cost the agency $1.0 billion, payments to acquiring firms would have been $0.5 billion higher. Total assistance costs therefore would have been $0.5 billion lower without the net worth program.

Regional variations. The earlier study suggested that a disproportionate share of the problems would occur in the Northeast and Midwest.[43] Experience over the past year has tended to confirm that assessment. Only 7 percent of the nation's savings and loan associations are in the Chicago and New York City metropolitan areas, but they constituted one-third of the assisted mergers in 1981 and 1982. This process is likely to continue, although at a somewhat lower rate as more and more of the problems are resolved.

Another observation from the earlier study suggested a high rate of mergers in Texas and Louisiana (FHLBB District 9). The new results

43. Ibid., pp. 34–36.

confirm the projection and show further that nearly all of these mergers will occur without assistance.

Characteristics of the nonviable firms. Two types of firms are most likely to be nonviable. Those not requiring merger assistance are small (assets of less than $50 million) and tend to have state rather than federal charters. They have relatively high operating costs but also reasonable prospects for growth, as they tend to be located in the South and West.

Firms requiring assistance to merge are larger than average (assets of more than $250 million) and are overwhelmingly concentrated in the Chicago and New York City areas. Their difficulties stem from slow or negative growth, low return on assets, high cost of funds, and low net worth.

Mutual Savings Banks

The model for savings banks was not updated for this paper. A comparison of the earlier results with recent experience suggests that, as with the savings and loans, unanticipated events have not seriously affected the original conclusions. The earlier results indicated losses continuing into 1984 under the pessimistic forecast.[44] Fourteen firms with assets of $22.6 billion were projected to require assistance; through 1982 there had been eleven assisted mergers involving assets of $15 billion. Total assistance costs to date have been $1.8 billion, and total costs therefore will probably be somewhat higher than the $2.1 billion calculated earlier.

Deposit Insurance Resources

With the implementation of the capital assistance program, additional financial claims will fall on the FSLIC and the FDIC. (Earlier proposals had specified the creation of a separate fund for this aid.) No additional funds were authorized, although an increase in the FSLIC's power to borrow from the Treasury was debated.[45] With the decline in interest rates after midyear, the resources of the FSLIC and the FDIC were deemed sufficient to meet needs arising over 1982–84, so the proposal was dropped.

44. Ibid., pp. 36–38.
45. Ibid., pp. 52–53.

This assessment appears to be valid. The adequacy of the FDIC fund has never been in doubt, given that agency's ability to assess additional premiums on (pay smaller rebates to) the healthy commercial banking industry to deal with the problems of a relatively few mutual savings bank failures. The outlook for the FSLIC, however, has not always appeared so sanguine.

It now seems apparent that current FSLIC resources will be adequate to meet all assistance requirements, barring a sharp and sustained rise in market interest rates. Insurance premium collections and investment earnings will roughly balance cash expenditures in the next few years. The corpus of the insurance fund will remain undiminished, helping to preserve public confidence in the viability of the fund, while substantial contingent and temporary claims are lodged against it.[46] Cumulative assistance to the savings and loan industry is projected to peak at $6.4 billion by 1984: total merger assistance of $5.9 billion, plus capital assistance of $1.2 billion in 1983 and $0.3 billion in 1984, less $1.0 billion of unrepaid capital assistance included in merger assistance, as previously described. At the beginning of 1981 the value of the FSLIC's assets was $6.6 billion.[47] To this should be added the Treasury borrowing authority ($0.7 billion) and the present value of 1981–84 premium and investment earnings (approximately $3 billion). Available resources of more than $10 billion continue to appear sufficient in light of the current economic outlook.

The Future of the Thrift Industry

Recent problems of the thrift industry resulted from regulations that limited its response to interest rate changes. Many of those controls have now been lifted. Savings and loan associations may now lend to a variety of borrowers on a short- or long-term basis; they can raise funds through new market-rate deposit instruments; changes in accounting techniques now permit firms to calculate their exposure to interest rate risks. Alternative mortgage loan instruments and the ability to deal in futures and options give the industry great freedom in avoiding the difficulties of the past.

Deregulation of financial markets also means more competition, not

46. See Carron, "Financial Crises."
47. This amount excludes the authority to require additional deposits by member associations. See Carron, *Plight of the Thrifts*, p. 52.

only from other local thrifts but also from savings conglomerates based in other states, commercial banks, and securities firms. Consumers over the past few years have lost their tolerance for below-market rates of return. And despite the recent hiatus, few believe that interest rate volatility is banished forever. What does this portend for the thrift industry?

First, despite lower interest rates and recent legislative changes, thrift institutions will experience adjustment difficulties for several years. Mergers of weak firms will continue at a high rate beyond 1983, leading to an industry of 2,500 firms or less. An adequate plan to facilitate this transition has been put in place. At the same time, the surviving firms can begin the process of asset and liability restructuring that is critical to their long-run viability.

Commercial banks will not be unaffected. The typical bank is even smaller and less efficient than the average thrift institution. These small banks will come under increasing pressure from larger banks and from savings and loan associations. A substantial consolidation of the banking industry can be expected on the heels of the current wave of thrift mergers.

There are more than 20,000 banks and thrifts in the United States (not including another 21,000 credit unions). This total could easily be reduced by half within the decade. Depository institutions that survive will be larger, more diverse, and less regulated than they are today. That prospect presents challenges both for government regulators and for the institutions themselves.

Restructuring the Institutions

Thrift institutions will use their new powers to reduce their vulnerability to swings in interest rates, but that implies learning new ways to earn a profit. Traditionally, savings and loan associations borrowed on a short-term basis and made long-term loans. Because short interest rates would average less than the initial long rate over the term of the loan, the institution made a profit. That was the return from maturity intermediation. Despite the problems of the past few years, it will be appropriate for thrifts to earn part of their income from this type of activity. They need to reduce, but not necessarily eliminate, the mismatch of maturities in their asset and liability portfolios. If an institution chooses to write only variable-rate loans or to hedge the mismatch of asset and liability maturities in the futures market, the

27

difference between long and short rates must accrue to the party taking the risk, not the thrift. And such floating-rate loans substitute a higher probability of default (credit risk) for the reduced risk of changes in the overall interest rate. Another option for the thrift is mortgage banking: selling new mortgages on the secondary market and deriving income from processing the application and collecting the payments. Such fees, determined at the outset, may in time prove insufficient to meet the costs of servicing the loan.

These alternative lines of business are well known to thrift managers. But the task is complicated by the need to reorient an existing institution with established practices and facilities. Thrifts developed in an era of regulation, and now they must compete in a deregulated environment.

Previously, government rules specified permissible investments, deposit accounts, interest rates, and business locations. The scope for innovation and enterprise was small, as the mark of success was the ability to comply with regulations. In the future, profitability will be a function of each firm's decisions rather than a result of forces working on the thrift industry collectively. Management will have more discretion, and the correct choices will be less obvious. Even the few entrepreneurial skills required under regulation must be reshaped for the new operating environment.

Under regulation, there was no price competition on the liability side of the balance sheet. Deposit instruments, denominations, maturities, and interest rates were set by federal agencies and imposed universally. What competition existed was based on service rather than price. Institutions offered more convenience and ancillary services at no charge to customers holding rate-controlled deposit balances. Extensive branch networks were constructed. Thrifts encouraged the small accounts that were costly to service but that built customer loyalty. This orientation has now become a serious drawback. Institutions must now pay market rates to attract deposits, so there is no surplus to finance extra service. It is difficult, however, to reduce service levels without losing customers. The new environment calls for fewer branch offices, each doing a larger volume of business. It may also mean that thrifts need to reevaluate their millions of small and now unprofitable depositors. Thrift institutions must learn to compete on the basis of price. That means explicit pricing—charging for each service while providing a high rate of return for the depositor who wants no frills.

As feeble as the competition was for liabilities, it was keen compared with that on the asset side. The institution had little control over the cost and quantity of funds coming in and was constrained in the permissible range of investments for those funds. So the marketing decision devolved to whether or not to make new mortgage loans at the going rate.

With deposit rate deregulation, that will change. Institutions need no longer rely on the traditional deposit base. With securities firms willing to act as brokers for funds to the thrifts, an institution can have exactly the quantity of new money it wants at the market price. That will place unfamiliar pressures on the investment decision. Although it may sound obvious, the challenge will be to decide what investments justify the acquisition of additional funds. The industry has not previously operated on this basis.

The new operating environment will continue to permit although not require thrifts to invest in residential mortgages. More mortgages will be sold in the secondary market to investors such as pension funds. Holdings of mortgages will be less concentrated in the thrift industry, but the availability of mortgage finance should not be greatly affected. The supply of savings in the economy relative to the investment demands of business, government, and consumers will be the principal determinants of the cost and availability of funds for housing.

Rationalizing Government's Role

Despite the reforms legislated in 1980 and 1982, the financial services industry is still subject to substantial regulation. The evolution of the thrift and banking industries will lead to further changes in the laws governing their activities. In an unsystematic although relentless manner, the entire structure of regulation constructed in the 1930s is being dismantled. For the most part, this is an appropriate response to changing conditions, but its essentially unplanned nature is cause for some concern.

The last vestiges of deposit rate regulation will soon be removed under existing statutes. New powers granted thrift institutions in the past few years will probably be expanded as the need arises. Certain changes in tax law will also be required to facilitate their use of the new powers. Interstate operations have been initiated for some thrift institutions as a means of resolving problems or avoiding business failures. The Federal Home Loan Bank Board has the authority to approve interstate acquisitions among healthy firms, and the likelihood is that the FHLBB will choose to do so. That will motivate Congress to address the fundamental prohibitions on interstate banking (the McFadden Act and the Douglas Amendment) that still purport to constrain it.

The organizational structure of federal financial regulation, which developed haphazardly over the past 120 years, has also come under review. There are at least ten different agencies that claim some jurisdiction over the financial services industry. In many instances the coverage overlaps, and it occasionally results in conflicts between regulators. This system may have been adequate in a time of strict industry regulation with little outright competition. And, while no one would have designed such a system if starting anew, it may have had some modest advantages in promoting specialization and diversity. But the financial industry now faces a different and unpredictable future. Existing weaknesses in the regulatory scheme will come under increasing pressure. The emerging economic environment demands corresponding changes in the regulatory structure. Rationalization must proceed in step with the anticipated restructuring of the banking and thrift industries.

Conclusions

In recent years high interest rates have triggered fears of financial crisis. Savings and loan associations and mutual savings banks were at the center of concern. In mid-1981 the most dire predictions of collapse seemed to be coming true.

The year 1982 was a critical one for the thrift industry. Lower interest rates after midyear and the enactment of major legislation in the fall indicated future improvement, but operating losses and failures surpassed the record levels of 1981.

Although many thrift institutions succumbed to their plight, the thrift industry has been rescued. Repercussions from the events of the past few years will continue to be felt, even with continued moderation of interest rates. The backlog of merger cases ensures further consolidation, and the net worth assistance program will require close supervision of large numbers of firms for up to ten years. But the crisis is over.

The problems of the thrift institutions were severe but manageable.

In the earlier study I stated that only a modest enhancement of the resources of the regulatory agencies would be required as long as interest rates came down even slightly from their 1981 levels. The appropriate legislative changes were implemented, and the anticipated decline in interest rates occurred. A more interventionist government policy could have involved substantial budgetary expenditures without materially improving the long-run outlook for the industry. Persistence of high interest rates into late 1982 would have exceeded the capacity of the existing system to deal with failing institutions. Fortunately no such breakdown occurred, and the resolution of difficulties proceeded in an orderly fashion.

The performance of the thrift industry in 1982 has been consistent with the forecast of 1981, but final judgments must await the full disposition of the problems. The estimates prepared for this paper demonstrate the effect on forecasts that refinements in modeling and changing economic and policy conditions can have. Nevertheless, the implications for industry structure and policy appear remarkably robust.

Several policy initiatives in 1982 bode well for the industry. The net worth assistance program, although not a substitute for merger, will permit a more deliberate process of consolidation with a broader array of choices for failing firms. It will, however, increase the long-run cost to the government of the consolidation process. The best reason for optimism about the future of the thrifts is the expansion of their asset and liability powers. Congress probably would not have expanded these powers had they not been linked to the assistance program. Yet, paradoxically, the opportunity these new powers offer the thrifts will ultimately be more vital to them than direct assistance.

31